45 Low-Sugar Sweet Treats Recipes for Home

By: Kelly Johnson

Table of Contents

- Sugar-Free Chocolate Avocado Mousse
- Almond Flour Blueberry Muffins
- Greek Yogurt Parfait with Berries
- Coconut Flour Lemon Bars
- Raspberry Chia Seed Pudding
- Dark Chocolate-dipped Strawberries
- No-Bake Peanut Butter Energy Bites
- Vanilla Almond Protein Cookies
- Apple Cinnamon Baked Oatmeal Cups
- Pumpkin Spice Protein Smoothie
- Sugar-Free Banana Bread
- Avocado Chocolate Truffles
- Coconut Chia Seed Energy Balls
- Cinnamon Apple Chips
- Low-Sugar Berry Sorbet
- Almond Butter Protein Fudge
- Zucchini Chocolate Chip Muffins
- Sugar-Free Mango Sorbet
- Peanut Butter Banana Oat Bars
- Lemon Poppy Seed Protein Pancakes
- Chocolate Avocado Popsicles
- No-Bake Coconut Cashew Bars
- Blueberry Almond Frozen Yogurt Bites
- Cranberry Walnut Energy Bites
- Chocolate Protein Ice Cream
- Pistachio Coconut Energy Balls
- Sugar-Free Strawberry Shortcake
- Almond Joy Protein Smoothie
- Pumpkin Spice Chia Pudding
- Raspberry Almond Thumbprint Cookies
- Greek Yogurt Cheesecake Bites
- Matcha Green Tea Energy Balls
- Chocolate Dipped Apricots
- Low-Sugar Apple Crisp
- Coconut Almond Joy Bars

- Vanilla Bean Panna Cotta
- Chocolate Almond Butter Banana Bites
- Berry Yogurt Popsicles
- Cinnamon Raisin Protein Cookies
- Avocado Lime Sorbet
- Walnut Dark Chocolate Clusters
- Peach Yogurt Parfait
- No-Bake Hazelnut Energy Bites
- Blueberry Cheesecake Bites
- Chia Seed Chocolate Pudding

Sugar-Free Chocolate Avocado Mousse

Ingredients:

- 2 ripe avocados
- 1/3 cup unsweetened cocoa powder
- 1/4 cup sugar-free sweetener (like erythritol or stevia)
- 1/4 cup almond milk or any milk of your choice
- 1 teaspoon vanilla extract
- A pinch of salt

Instructions:

Cut the avocados in half, remove the pits, and scoop the flesh into a blender or food processor.
Add cocoa powder, sugar-free sweetener, almond milk, vanilla extract, and a pinch of salt to the blender.
Blend the ingredients until smooth and creamy, scraping down the sides of the blender or food processor as needed.
Taste the mousse and adjust sweetness if necessary by adding more sweetener.
Once the mixture is smooth and well combined, transfer the mousse to serving bowls or glasses.
Refrigerate for at least 1-2 hours to allow the mousse to set.
Before serving, you can garnish with fresh berries, chopped nuts, or a dollop of whipped cream if desired.

Enjoy your delicious Sugar-Free Chocolate Avocado Mousse!

Almond Flour Blueberry Muffins

Ingredients:

- 2 cups almond flour
- 1/4 cup coconut flour
- 1/2 teaspoon baking soda
- 1/4 teaspoon salt
- 3 large eggs
- 1/4 cup melted coconut oil or butter
- 1/3 cup sugar-free sweetener (such as erythritol or stevia)
- 1 teaspoon vanilla extract
- 1/2 cup unsweetened almond milk
- 1 cup fresh or frozen blueberries

Instructions:

Preheat your oven to 350°F (175°C). Line a muffin tin with paper liners or grease the cups.
In a large mixing bowl, combine almond flour, coconut flour, baking soda, and salt. Mix well.
In another bowl, whisk together the eggs, melted coconut oil or butter, sugar-free sweetener, vanilla extract, and almond milk until well combined.
Add the wet ingredients to the dry ingredients and stir until just combined. Be careful not to overmix.
Gently fold in the blueberries into the batter.
Spoon the batter into the prepared muffin cups, filling each about 2/3 full.
Bake in the preheated oven for 20-25 minutes or until a toothpick inserted into the center of a muffin comes out clean.
Allow the muffins to cool in the tin for 5 minutes, then transfer them to a wire rack to cool completely.
Enjoy your delicious Almond Flour Blueberry Muffins!

Feel free to adjust sweetness or add a touch of lemon zest for extra flavor if desired.

Greek Yogurt Parfait with Berries

Ingredients:

- 1 cup Greek yogurt (unsweetened)
- 2 tablespoons honey or maple syrup (optional, for sweetness)
- 1 cup mixed berries (strawberries, blueberries, raspberries)
- 1/4 cup granola (choose a low-sugar or sugar-free option if desired)
- Fresh mint leaves for garnish (optional)

Instructions:

In a bowl, mix the Greek yogurt with honey or maple syrup if you desire additional sweetness. Adjust the sweetness according to your taste.
Wash and prepare the berries. If using strawberries, slice them into smaller pieces.
In serving glasses or bowls, layer the Greek yogurt, followed by a layer of mixed berries.
Sprinkle a layer of granola on top of the berries.
Repeat the layers until you reach the top of the glass, finishing with a dollop of Greek yogurt.
Garnish with fresh mint leaves if desired.
Serve immediately and enjoy your delicious Greek Yogurt Parfait with Berries!

This parfait is not only visually appealing but also a nutritious and satisfying treat. Feel free to customize it by adding other fruits, nuts, or seeds according to your preferences.

Coconut Flour Lemon Bars

Ingredients:

For the Crust:

- 1/2 cup coconut flour
- 1/4 cup almond flour
- 1/4 cup melted coconut oil
- 2 tablespoons sugar-free sweetener (such as erythritol or stevia)
- A pinch of salt

For the Lemon Filling:

- 4 large eggs
- 1/2 cup fresh lemon juice (about 3-4 lemons)
- 1 teaspoon lemon zest
- 1/2 cup coconut flour
- 1/2 cup sugar-free sweetener
- 1/4 cup melted coconut oil
- 1/2 teaspoon baking powder
- A pinch of salt

Instructions:

Preheat your oven to 350°F (175°C). Line an 8x8 inch (20x20 cm) baking pan with parchment paper, leaving some overhang for easy removal.
In a bowl, mix together the coconut flour, almond flour, melted coconut oil, sugar-free sweetener, and a pinch of salt for the crust until well combined.
Press the crust mixture evenly into the bottom of the prepared baking pan.
Bake the crust in the preheated oven for about 10-12 minutes or until lightly golden. Remove from the oven and let it cool while you prepare the lemon filling.
For the lemon filling, whisk together the eggs, fresh lemon juice, lemon zest, coconut flour, sugar-free sweetener, melted coconut oil, baking powder, and a pinch of salt until smooth.
Pour the lemon filling over the cooled crust, spreading it evenly.

Bake in the oven for 20-25 minutes or until the edges are set, and the center is slightly firm.

Allow the lemon bars to cool in the pan, then refrigerate for at least 2 hours or until completely chilled.

Once chilled, lift the bars out of the pan using the parchment paper overhang. Cut into squares or bars.

Optionally, dust the tops with a little coconut flour or powdered sweetener before serving.

Enjoy your Coconut Flour Lemon Bars!

These bars are a delightful combination of tangy lemon flavor and a coconut-flour-based crust, making them a delicious low-sugar treat.

Raspberry Chia Seed Pudding

Ingredients:

- 1/2 cup chia seeds
- 2 cups unsweetened almond milk (or any milk of your choice)
- 1 teaspoon vanilla extract
- 2 tablespoons sugar-free sweetener (such as erythritol or stevia), or to taste
- 1 cup fresh raspberries (or thawed frozen raspberries)
- Additional raspberries for garnish (optional)

Instructions:

In a bowl, combine chia seeds, almond milk, vanilla extract, and sugar-free sweetener. Mix well.

Let the mixture sit for about 5 minutes, then stir again to make sure the chia seeds are evenly distributed.

Cover the bowl and refrigerate for at least 2 hours or overnight. During this time, the chia seeds will absorb the liquid and create a pudding-like consistency.

In a blender or food processor, puree the fresh raspberries until smooth. If using frozen raspberries, you can thaw them and then blend.

Once the chia seed mixture has set, give it a good stir. Layer the chia pudding and raspberry puree in serving glasses or jars.

Repeat the layers until you reach the top, finishing with a dollop of raspberry puree.

Garnish with additional fresh raspberries if desired.

Serve chilled and enjoy your delicious Raspberry Chia Seed Pudding!

This pudding is not only tasty but also packed with fiber and healthy fats from chia seeds, making it a nutritious and satisfying dessert or breakfast option.

Dark Chocolate-dipped Strawberries

Ingredients:

- 1 pound fresh strawberries, washed and dried
- 6 ounces dark chocolate (70% cocoa or higher), chopped
- 1 tablespoon coconut oil
- Optional toppings: chopped nuts, shredded coconut, or sea salt

Instructions:

Line a baking sheet with parchment paper.
In a heatproof bowl, combine the chopped dark chocolate and coconut oil.
Place the bowl over a pot of simmering water (double boiler) or melt the chocolate in the microwave using 20-second intervals, stirring between each interval until smooth.
Hold each strawberry by the stem and dip it into the melted chocolate, coating it evenly.
Allow any excess chocolate to drip off, then place the dipped strawberry on the prepared parchment paper.
If desired, sprinkle the dipped strawberries with chopped nuts, shredded coconut, or a pinch of sea salt while the chocolate is still wet.
Repeat the process with the remaining strawberries.
Place the baking sheet in the refrigerator for about 30 minutes or until the chocolate has hardened.
Once the chocolate is set, transfer the dark chocolate-dipped strawberries to a serving plate.
Serve and enjoy your delicious Dark Chocolate-dipped Strawberries!

These chocolate-dipped strawberries make for a delightful and healthier dessert option, as dark chocolate contains antioxidants and strawberries are rich in vitamins.

No-Bake Peanut Butter Energy Bites

Ingredients:

- 1 cup old-fashioned oats
- 1/2 cup creamy peanut butter
- 1/3 cup honey or maple syrup
- 1 cup unsweetened shredded coconut
- 1/2 cup ground flaxseed
- 1 teaspoon vanilla extract
- A pinch of salt
- Optional: 1/3 cup mini chocolate chips or chopped nuts

Instructions:

In a large mixing bowl, combine the oats, peanut butter, honey or maple syrup, shredded coconut, ground flaxseed, vanilla extract, and a pinch of salt.
If desired, add mini chocolate chips or chopped nuts to the mixture.
Stir the ingredients until well combined. The mixture should be sticky and easy to form into balls.
With clean hands, take about a tablespoon of the mixture and roll it into a ball. Repeat until all the mixture is used.
Place the energy bites on a baking sheet lined with parchment paper.
Refrigerate the energy bites for at least 30 minutes to firm up.
Once chilled, transfer the energy bites to an airtight container and store them in the refrigerator.
Enjoy your No-Bake Peanut Butter Energy Bites as a quick and nutritious snack!

These energy bites are not only delicious but also packed with fiber, healthy fats, and protein, making them a perfect on-the-go snack or pre/post-workout treat.

Vanilla Almond Protein Cookies

Ingredients:

- 1 cup almond flour
- 1/2 cup vanilla protein powder
- 1/4 cup coconut flour
- 1/4 teaspoon baking soda
- 1/4 teaspoon salt
- 1/2 cup unsalted butter, softened
- 1/4 cup sugar-free sweetener (such as erythritol or stevia)
- 1 large egg
- 1 teaspoon vanilla extract
- 1/2 cup chopped almonds

Instructions:

Preheat your oven to 350°F (175°C) and line a baking sheet with parchment paper.
In a bowl, whisk together the almond flour, vanilla protein powder, coconut flour, baking soda, and salt.
In a separate large bowl, cream together the softened butter and sugar-free sweetener until light and fluffy.
Add the egg and vanilla extract to the butter mixture and mix until well combined.
Gradually add the dry ingredients to the wet ingredients, mixing until a dough forms.
Fold in the chopped almonds until evenly distributed throughout the dough.
Scoop out tablespoon-sized portions of dough and roll them into balls. Place the balls on the prepared baking sheet, spacing them about 2 inches apart.
Flatten each cookie slightly with the back of a fork or your fingertips.
Bake in the preheated oven for 10-12 minutes or until the edges are golden brown.
Allow the cookies to cool on the baking sheet for a few minutes before transferring them to a wire rack to cool completely.
Enjoy your Vanilla Almond Protein Cookies!

These cookies are a tasty and protein-packed treat, perfect for satisfying your sweet cravings while providing a boost of energy. Adjust sweetness or add a touch of cinnamon for extra flavor if desired.

Apple Cinnamon Baked Oatmeal Cups

Ingredients:

- 2 cups old-fashioned oats
- 1 teaspoon baking powder
- 1 teaspoon ground cinnamon
- 1/4 teaspoon salt
- 1 1/2 cups unsweetened almond milk (or any milk of your choice)
- 1/4 cup maple syrup or honey
- 1 large egg, beaten
- 1 teaspoon vanilla extract
- 2 medium-sized apples, peeled, cored, and finely diced
- 1/4 cup chopped nuts (such as walnuts or pecans), optional

Instructions:

Preheat your oven to 350°F (175°C). Grease a muffin tin or line it with paper liners.
In a large mixing bowl, combine the oats, baking powder, ground cinnamon, and salt.
In a separate bowl, whisk together the almond milk, maple syrup or honey, beaten egg, and vanilla extract.
Pour the wet ingredients into the bowl with the dry ingredients and mix until well combined.
Fold in the diced apples and chopped nuts, if using.
Let the mixture sit for a few minutes to allow the oats to absorb some of the liquid.
Spoon the oatmeal mixture into the prepared muffin tin, filling each cup almost to the top.
Bake in the preheated oven for 20-25 minutes or until the tops are golden brown and a toothpick inserted into the center comes out clean.
Allow the oatmeal cups to cool in the muffin tin for a few minutes before transferring them to a wire rack to cool completely.
Serve and enjoy your Apple Cinnamon Baked Oatmeal Cups!

These oatmeal cups are not only delicious but also make a convenient and portable breakfast option. You can customize them by adding dried fruit, seeds, or a drizzle of nut butter if desired.

Pumpkin Spice Protein Smoothie

Ingredients:

- 1/2 cup canned pumpkin puree
- 1/2 banana, frozen
- 1 cup unsweetened almond milk (or any milk of your choice)
- 1 scoop vanilla protein powder
- 1/2 teaspoon pumpkin spice blend (or a mixture of cinnamon, nutmeg, and ginger)
- 1 tablespoon chia seeds (optional)
- Ice cubes (optional)
- Sweetener to taste (such as honey or maple syrup)

Instructions:

In a blender, combine the canned pumpkin puree, frozen banana, almond milk, vanilla protein powder, pumpkin spice blend, and chia seeds.
Blend on high speed until the smoothie reaches your desired consistency. If the smoothie is too thick, you can add more almond milk.
Taste the smoothie and add sweetener if needed, depending on your preference.
If you prefer a colder smoothie, you can add ice cubes and blend again until smooth.
Pour the smoothie into a glass and garnish with a sprinkle of pumpkin spice on top if desired.
Enjoy your Pumpkin Spice Protein Smoothie as a delicious and nutritious fall-inspired treat!

Feel free to customize this smoothie by adding a handful of spinach or kale for extra greens, or adjusting the spice levels to suit your taste.

Sugar-Free Banana Bread

Ingredients:

- 3 ripe bananas, mashed
- 1/3 cup unsweetened applesauce
- 1/4 cup melted coconut oil or butter
- 2 large eggs
- 1 teaspoon vanilla extract
- 2 cups almond flour
- 1 teaspoon baking soda
- 1/2 teaspoon baking powder
- 1/2 teaspoon ground cinnamon
- 1/4 teaspoon salt
- 1/2 cup chopped nuts (such as walnuts or pecans), optional

Instructions:

Preheat your oven to 350°F (175°C). Grease a standard-sized loaf pan or line it with parchment paper.
In a large mixing bowl, mash the ripe bananas.
Add the applesauce, melted coconut oil or butter, eggs, and vanilla extract to the mashed bananas. Mix until well combined.
In a separate bowl, whisk together the almond flour, baking soda, baking powder, ground cinnamon, and salt.
Gradually add the dry ingredients to the banana mixture, stirring until just combined. Be careful not to overmix.
If desired, fold in chopped nuts.
Pour the batter into the prepared loaf pan, spreading it evenly.
Bake in the preheated oven for 50-60 minutes or until a toothpick inserted into the center comes out clean.
Allow the banana bread to cool in the pan for 10 minutes, then transfer it to a wire rack to cool completely.
Slice and enjoy your Sugar-Free Banana Bread!

This banana bread is naturally sweetened by the ripe bananas, and the absence of added sugar makes it a healthier option. Feel free to customize by adding a touch of cinnamon, nutmeg, or vanilla for extra flavor.

Avocado Chocolate Truffles

Ingredients:

- 2 ripe avocados
- 1/2 cup dark chocolate chips or chopped dark chocolate (70% cocoa or higher)
- 2 tablespoons unsweetened cocoa powder
- 1-2 tablespoons maple syrup or sweetener of choice
- 1 teaspoon vanilla extract
- A pinch of salt
- Optional coatings: shredded coconut, chopped nuts, cocoa powder, or melted dark chocolate for dipping

Instructions:

Melt the dark chocolate in a heatproof bowl over a pot of simmering water (double boiler) or in the microwave using 20-second intervals, stirring between each interval until smooth. Allow it to cool slightly.
Cut the avocados in half, remove the pits, and scoop the flesh into a blender or food processor.
Add the melted chocolate, cocoa powder, maple syrup, vanilla extract, and a pinch of salt to the blender with the avocados.
Blend the mixture until smooth and creamy, scraping down the sides of the blender or food processor as needed.
Taste the mixture and adjust the sweetness if necessary by adding more maple syrup.
Transfer the chocolate-avocado mixture to a bowl and refrigerate for about 30 minutes to firm up.
Once the mixture is firm, scoop out small portions and roll them into bite-sized truffles. If the mixture is too sticky, you can refrigerate it for a bit longer.
Roll the truffles in your choice of coatings, such as shredded coconut, chopped nuts, cocoa powder, or dip them in melted dark chocolate.
Place the truffles on a parchment-lined tray and refrigerate for another 30 minutes to set.
Once set, transfer the truffles to an airtight container and store them in the refrigerator.
Enjoy your delicious Avocado Chocolate Truffles!

These truffles are not only rich and indulgent but also benefit from the creamy texture that avocado provides. Feel free to get creative with coatings and toppings based on your preferences.

Coconut Chia Seed Energy Balls

Ingredients:

- 1 cup pitted dates
- 1 cup unsweetened shredded coconut
- 1/4 cup chia seeds
- 1/4 cup almond butter or any nut butter of your choice
- 1 teaspoon vanilla extract
- A pinch of salt
- Additional shredded coconut for rolling (optional)

Instructions:

In a food processor, combine dates, shredded coconut, chia seeds, almond butter, vanilla extract, and a pinch of salt.
Process the mixture until it forms a sticky, uniform dough. If the mixture is too dry, you can add a small amount of water, one tablespoon at a time.
Scoop out small portions of the dough and roll them into bite-sized balls between your hands.
If desired, roll the energy balls in additional shredded coconut to coat them.
Place the energy balls on a parchment-lined tray or plate.
Refrigerate the energy balls for at least 30 minutes to firm up.
Once set, transfer the energy balls to an airtight container and store them in the refrigerator.
Enjoy your Coconut Chia Seed Energy Balls as a quick and nutritious snack!

These energy balls are not only delicious but also packed with fiber, healthy fats, and protein. They make for a convenient and portable snack, and you can customize them by adding other ingredients like nuts, seeds, or dried fruit if desired.

Cinnamon Apple Chips

Ingredients:

- 2-3 large apples (choose a sweet variety like Honeycrisp or Gala)
- 1-2 teaspoons ground cinnamon
- Optional: 1-2 teaspoons sugar or sweetener of choice

Instructions:

Preheat your oven to 200°F (93°C). Line two baking sheets with parchment paper. Wash and thinly slice the apples using a sharp knife or a mandolin slicer. Aim for slices about 1/8-inch thick.

In a bowl, toss the apple slices with ground cinnamon. If you prefer a sweeter taste, you can add sugar or a sweetener at this point.

Arrange the apple slices in a single layer on the prepared baking sheets, ensuring they do not overlap.

Bake in the preheated oven for 1.5 to 2 hours, flipping the slices halfway through, or until the apple chips are dried and slightly crispy. Keep an eye on them towards the end to prevent burning.

Remove from the oven and let the apple chips cool on the baking sheets. They will continue to crisp up as they cool.

Once cooled, store the cinnamon apple chips in an airtight container.

Enjoy your homemade Cinnamon Apple Chips as a healthy and flavorful snack!

These apple chips are a great alternative to store-bought snacks and are perfect for satisfying sweet cravings without added sugars. Adjust the cinnamon and sweetness levels according to your taste preferences.

Low-Sugar Berry Sorbet

Ingredients:

- 3 cups mixed berries (strawberries, blueberries, raspberries)
- 1/4 cup water
- 2 tablespoons lemon juice
- 2-3 tablespoons sugar-free sweetener (such as erythritol or stevia), or to taste
- Optional: Fresh mint leaves for garnish

Instructions:

Wash the mixed berries and remove any stems.
In a blender or food processor, combine the mixed berries, water, lemon juice, and sugar-free sweetener.
Blend the ingredients until smooth. Taste the mixture and adjust the sweetness if needed by adding more sweetener.
Strain the berry mixture through a fine-mesh sieve to remove seeds and pulp. This step is optional if you prefer a smoother sorbet.
Pour the strained mixture into a shallow, freezer-safe dish.
Place the dish in the freezer and let it freeze for about 1-2 hours.
After the initial freezing, use a fork to scrape and fluff the sorbet, breaking up any ice crystals. Return it to the freezer.
Repeat the scraping process every 30 minutes for the next 2-3 hours, or until the sorbet reaches the desired consistency.
Once the sorbet is firm but scoopable, it's ready to serve.
Scoop the low-sugar berry sorbet into bowls or cones, garnish with fresh mint leaves if desired, and enjoy!

This low-sugar berry sorbet is a refreshing and guilt-free treat, perfect for satisfying your sweet tooth without the added sugars commonly found in store-bought sorbets.

Almond Butter Protein Fudge

Ingredients:

- 1 cup almond butter
- 1/4 cup coconut oil, melted
- 1/4 cup protein powder (vanilla or chocolate flavor)
- 2 tablespoons sugar-free sweetener (such as erythritol or stevia), or to taste
- 1 teaspoon vanilla extract
- A pinch of salt
- Optional: Chopped nuts or shredded coconut for texture

Instructions:

In a microwave-safe bowl or on the stovetop, melt the coconut oil.
In a mixing bowl, combine the almond butter, melted coconut oil, protein powder, sugar-free sweetener, vanilla extract, and a pinch of salt.
Mix the ingredients until smooth and well combined. Taste the mixture and adjust sweetness if needed.
If desired, fold in chopped nuts or shredded coconut for added texture.
Line a small square or rectangular dish with parchment paper.
Pour the almond butter protein fudge mixture into the prepared dish, spreading it evenly.
Place the dish in the refrigerator and let it set for at least 2-3 hours, or until firm.
Once set, lift the fudge out of the dish using the parchment paper, and cut it into small squares.
Store the almond butter protein fudge in an airtight container in the refrigerator.
Enjoy your Almond Butter Protein Fudge as a delicious and protein-packed treat!

This fudge is a great way to satisfy your sweet cravings while incorporating protein into your diet. Feel free to experiment with different flavors of protein powder or add your favorite mix-ins for variation.

Zucchini Chocolate Chip Muffins

Ingredients:

- 1 1/2 cups shredded zucchini (about 1 medium-sized zucchini)
- 1 1/2 cups all-purpose flour or a combination of all-purpose and whole wheat flour
- 1/2 cup unsweetened cocoa powder
- 1 teaspoon baking powder
- 1/2 teaspoon baking soda
- 1/2 teaspoon salt
- 1/2 cup coconut oil or vegetable oil
- 1/2 cup sugar or sugar substitute (such as erythritol)
- 2 large eggs
- 1 teaspoon vanilla extract
- 1/2 cup plain Greek yogurt or sour cream
- 1/2 cup chocolate chips (dark or semi-sweet)

Instructions:

Preheat your oven to 350°F (175°C). Line a muffin tin with paper liners or grease the cups.
Shred the zucchini using a grater, and then squeeze out any excess moisture using a clean kitchen towel.
In a medium-sized bowl, whisk together the flour, cocoa powder, baking powder, baking soda, and salt.
In a large bowl, beat together the coconut oil, sugar, eggs, and vanilla extract until well combined.
Add the shredded zucchini to the wet ingredients and mix well.
Gradually add the dry ingredients to the wet ingredients, mixing until just combined.
Fold in the Greek yogurt or sour cream until the batter is smooth.
Gently fold in the chocolate chips.
Spoon the batter into the prepared muffin cups, filling each about 2/3 full.
Bake in the preheated oven for 18-20 minutes or until a toothpick inserted into the center of a muffin comes out clean.
Allow the muffins to cool in the tin for 5 minutes, then transfer them to a wire rack to cool completely.
Enjoy your Zucchini Chocolate Chip Muffins as a tasty and slightly healthier treat!

These muffins are a great way to sneak in some veggies while enjoying a delicious chocolatey treat. Adjust sweetness or use sugar substitutes for a lower sugar option if desired.

Sugar-Free Mango Sorbet

Ingredients:

- 4 cups frozen mango chunks
- 1/4 cup water
- 2 tablespoons lemon or lime juice
- 2-3 tablespoons sugar-free sweetener (such as erythritol or stevia), or to taste
- Optional: Fresh mint leaves for garnish

Instructions:

In a blender or food processor, combine the frozen mango chunks, water, lemon or lime juice, and sugar-free sweetener.
Blend the mixture until smooth and creamy. If it's too thick, you can add a bit more water, one tablespoon at a time.
Taste the sorbet mixture and adjust the sweetness if needed by adding more sugar-free sweetener.
Once the sorbet mixture is smooth and to your liking, transfer it to a shallow, freezer-safe dish.
Spread the sorbet evenly in the dish and smooth the top.
Cover the dish with plastic wrap or a lid and place it in the freezer.
Let the sorbet freeze for at least 2-3 hours or until firm.
Before serving, let the sorbet sit at room temperature for a few minutes to soften slightly.
Use an ice cream scoop or spoon to scoop the sugar-free mango sorbet into bowls or cones.
Garnish with fresh mint leaves if desired and enjoy!

This sugar-free mango sorbet is a refreshing and guilt-free dessert. Feel free to experiment with other frozen fruits or add a splash of coconut milk for extra creaminess if you like.

Peanut Butter Banana Oat Bars

Ingredients:

- 2 ripe bananas, mashed
- 1/2 cup creamy peanut butter
- 1/4 cup honey or maple syrup
- 1 teaspoon vanilla extract
- 2 cups old-fashioned oats
- 1/2 teaspoon cinnamon
- 1/4 teaspoon salt
- 1/2 cup chopped nuts (such as walnuts or almonds), optional
- 1/4 cup chocolate chips, optional

Instructions:

Preheat your oven to 350°F (175°C). Grease or line an 8x8 inch (20x20 cm) baking pan with parchment paper.
In a large mixing bowl, mash the ripe bananas.
Add the peanut butter, honey or maple syrup, and vanilla extract to the mashed bananas. Mix until well combined.
In a separate bowl, combine the oats, cinnamon, and salt.
Gradually add the dry ingredients to the banana mixture, stirring until everything is well incorporated.
If desired, fold in chopped nuts and chocolate chips.
Press the mixture into the prepared baking pan, ensuring it's evenly distributed and pressed down.
Bake in the preheated oven for 20-25 minutes or until the edges are golden brown.
Allow the bars to cool in the pan for 10 minutes, then transfer them to a wire rack to cool completely.
Once cooled, cut the bars into squares or rectangles.
Enjoy your Peanut Butter Banana Oat Bars as a delicious and wholesome snack!

These bars are a great combination of peanut butter, banana, and oats, making them a satisfying and energy-boosting treat. Feel free to customize by adding dried fruit or seeds if desired.

Lemon Poppy Seed Protein Pancakes

Ingredients:

- 1 cup whole wheat flour or oat flour
- 1 scoop vanilla protein powder
- 1 tablespoon poppy seeds
- 1 teaspoon baking powder
- 1/2 teaspoon baking soda
- 1/4 teaspoon salt
- 1 cup unsweetened almond milk or any milk of your choice
- 1 large egg
- 2 tablespoons lemon juice
- Zest of 1 lemon
- 2 tablespoons honey or maple syrup
- 1 teaspoon vanilla extract
- Cooking spray or oil for the pan

Instructions:

In a large mixing bowl, whisk together the whole wheat flour or oat flour, vanilla protein powder, poppy seeds, baking powder, baking soda, and salt.
In a separate bowl, whisk together the almond milk, egg, lemon juice, lemon zest, honey or maple syrup, and vanilla extract.
Pour the wet ingredients into the dry ingredients and stir until just combined. Do not overmix; it's okay if there are a few lumps.
Let the batter sit for a couple of minutes to allow the poppy seeds to soften slightly.
Preheat a griddle or non-stick pan over medium heat. Lightly coat it with cooking spray or a small amount of oil.
Pour 1/4 cup of batter onto the griddle for each pancake.
Cook until bubbles form on the surface, then flip and cook the other side until golden brown.
Repeat until all the batter is used, adding more oil or cooking spray to the pan as needed.
Serve the Lemon Poppy Seed Protein Pancakes with your favorite toppings, such as fresh berries, a drizzle of honey, or a dollop of Greek yogurt.
Enjoy your delicious and protein-packed pancakes!

These pancakes offer a delightful combination of citrusy flavor from the lemon and the crunch of poppy seeds, making them a tasty and nutritious breakfast option.

Chocolate Avocado Popsicles

Ingredients:

- 2 ripe avocados, peeled and pitted
- 1/2 cup unsweetened cocoa powder
- 1/2 cup coconut milk (or any milk of your choice)
- 1/4 cup honey or maple syrup (adjust to taste)
- 1 teaspoon vanilla extract
- A pinch of salt
- Optional: Chocolate chips or chopped nuts for added texture

Instructions:

In a blender or food processor, combine the ripe avocados, cocoa powder, coconut milk, honey or maple syrup, vanilla extract, and a pinch of salt.
Blend the mixture until smooth and creamy. Taste and adjust the sweetness if needed.
If desired, fold in chocolate chips or chopped nuts for added texture.
Pour the chocolate avocado mixture into popsicle molds, leaving a little space at the top for expansion.
Insert popsicle sticks into the molds.
Freeze the popsicles for at least 4-6 hours or until completely set.
Once frozen, run the popsicle molds under warm water for a few seconds to help release the popsicles.
Remove the popsicles from the molds and enjoy your Chocolate Avocado Popsicles!

These popsicles are not only delicious but also a healthier alternative to traditional ice pops, thanks to the creamy texture provided by avocados and the natural sweetness from honey or maple syrup.

No-Bake Coconut Cashew Bars

Ingredients:

For the Base:

- 1 cup cashews
- 1 cup shredded coconut (unsweetened)
- 1/4 cup coconut oil, melted
- 2 tablespoons honey or maple syrup
- A pinch of salt

For the Topping:

- 1/2 cup coconut oil, melted
- 1/4 cup cashew butter (or any nut butter of your choice)
- 2 tablespoons honey or maple syrup
- 1 teaspoon vanilla extract
- A pinch of salt

Instructions:

For the Base:

In a food processor, combine cashews, shredded coconut, melted coconut oil, honey or maple syrup, and a pinch of salt.
Process the ingredients until they form a sticky, crumbly mixture.
Line a square or rectangular dish with parchment paper, leaving some overhang for easy removal.
Press the cashew-coconut mixture into the bottom of the lined dish, creating an even layer.
Place the dish in the freezer while you prepare the topping.

For the Topping:

In a bowl, whisk together melted coconut oil, cashew butter, honey or maple syrup, vanilla extract, and a pinch of salt until smooth.
Pour the topping over the chilled base layer in the dish.
Return the dish to the freezer and let it set for at least 2-3 hours or until completely firm.

Once set, use the parchment paper overhang to lift the bars out of the dish.
Place the bars on a cutting board and use a sharp knife to cut them into squares or bars.
Store the No-Bake Coconut Cashew Bars in the refrigerator until ready to serve.
Enjoy these delicious and wholesome bars!

These no-bake bars are not only easy to make but also a great combination of coconut and cashew flavors, providing a satisfying and nutritious snack or dessert option.

Blueberry Almond Frozen Yogurt Bites

Ingredients:

- 1 cup Greek yogurt (plain or vanilla)
- 1/2 cup fresh or frozen blueberries
- 2 tablespoons honey or maple syrup
- 1/4 cup almonds, chopped
- 1/2 teaspoon vanilla extract

Instructions:

In a bowl, combine Greek yogurt, honey or maple syrup, and vanilla extract. Mix until well combined.
Gently fold in the blueberries and chopped almonds into the yogurt mixture.
Line a mini-muffin tin with silicone or paper liners.
Spoon the yogurt mixture into each cup, filling them almost to the top.
Use a spatula or spoon to smooth the tops of the yogurt mixture in each cup.
Place the mini-muffin tin in the freezer and let the yogurt bites freeze for at least 3-4 hours or until firm.
Once the bites are frozen, remove them from the muffin tin.
Let the frozen yogurt bites sit at room temperature for a minute or two before serving to slightly soften.
Enjoy your Blueberry Almond Frozen Yogurt Bites as a refreshing and nutritious frozen treat!

These frozen yogurt bites are not only delicious but also provide a burst of antioxidants from the blueberries and a crunch from the almonds. Adjust sweetness according to your taste preferences.

Cranberry Walnut Energy Bites

Ingredients:

- 1 cup old-fashioned oats
- 1/2 cup dried cranberries
- 1/2 cup chopped walnuts
- 1/4 cup ground flaxseed
- 1/4 cup honey or maple syrup
- 1/2 cup almond butter or any nut butter of your choice
- 1 teaspoon vanilla extract
- A pinch of salt
- Optional: Shredded coconut for rolling

Instructions:

In a food processor, combine oats, dried cranberries, chopped walnuts, and ground flaxseed. Pulse until the mixture is finely chopped.
Transfer the mixture to a mixing bowl.
Add honey or maple syrup, almond butter, vanilla extract, and a pinch of salt to the bowl.
Stir the ingredients until well combined. If the mixture seems too dry, you can add a bit more honey or almond butter.
Place the mixture in the refrigerator for about 30 minutes to make it easier to handle.
After chilling, take small portions of the mixture and roll them into bite-sized balls using your hands.
Optional: Roll the energy bites in shredded coconut for an extra layer of flavor and texture.
Place the energy bites on a parchment-lined tray or plate.
Refrigerate the energy bites for at least 30 minutes to firm up.
Once set, transfer the energy bites to an airtight container and store them in the refrigerator.
Enjoy your Cranberry Walnut Energy Bites as a delicious and nutritious snack!

These energy bites are packed with wholesome ingredients, providing a combination of fiber, healthy fats, and natural sweetness. They make for a convenient and energy-boosting snack on the go.

Chocolate Protein Ice Cream

Ingredients:

- 2 large ripe bananas, sliced and frozen
- 1/4 cup unsweetened cocoa powder
- 1/4 cup chocolate protein powder
- 1/2 cup unsweetened almond milk (or any milk of your choice)
- 1 teaspoon vanilla extract
- Optional: Sweetener of choice (such as honey or maple syrup), to taste
- Optional toppings: Chopped nuts, shredded coconut, or dark chocolate chips

Instructions:

Make sure to freeze the sliced bananas for at least 4 hours or overnight.
In a blender or food processor, combine the frozen banana slices, cocoa powder, chocolate protein powder, almond milk, and vanilla extract.
Blend the mixture until smooth and creamy. You may need to stop and scrape down the sides of the blender or food processor a few times.
Taste the ice cream base and add sweetener if desired, depending on your preference.
Continue blending until the mixture reaches a soft-serve consistency.
If you prefer a firmer texture, transfer the ice cream to a container and freeze for an additional 1-2 hours.
Once the chocolate protein ice cream is set to your liking, scoop it into bowls or cones.
Optionally, top the ice cream with chopped nuts, shredded coconut, or dark chocolate chips.
Enjoy your homemade Chocolate Protein Ice Cream as a guilt-free and protein-packed dessert!

This chocolate protein ice cream is a healthier alternative to traditional ice cream, providing a dose of protein while satisfying your chocolate cravings. Feel free to customize it with your favorite toppings or mix-ins.

Pistachio Coconut Energy Balls

Ingredients:

- 1 cup shelled pistachios
- 1 cup shredded coconut (unsweetened)
- 1 cup dates, pitted
- 2 tablespoons coconut oil
- 1 teaspoon vanilla extract
- A pinch of salt
- Additional shredded coconut for rolling (optional)

Instructions:

In a food processor, combine shelled pistachios, shredded coconut, dates, coconut oil, vanilla extract, and a pinch of salt.
Process the ingredients until the mixture forms a sticky and uniform dough. If it's too dry, you can add a bit more coconut oil.
Scoop out small portions of the mixture and roll them into bite-sized balls using your hands.
Optional: Roll the energy balls in additional shredded coconut for an extra layer of flavor.
Place the energy balls on a parchment-lined tray or plate.
Refrigerate the energy balls for at least 30 minutes to firm up.
Once set, transfer the energy balls to an airtight container and store them in the refrigerator.
Enjoy your Pistachio Coconut Energy Balls as a delicious and nutritious snack!

These energy balls are packed with the goodness of pistachios, coconut, and dates, providing a combination of healthy fats, fiber, and natural sweetness. They make for a convenient and energy-boosting snack on the go.

Sugar-Free Strawberry Shortcake

Ingredients:

For the Shortcakes:

- 2 cups almond flour
- 1/4 cup coconut flour
- 1/4 cup sugar-free sweetener (such as erythritol or stevia)
- 1 teaspoon baking powder
- 1/2 teaspoon baking soda
- 1/4 teaspoon salt
- 1/2 cup unsalted butter, melted
- 3 large eggs
- 1 teaspoon vanilla extract

For the Topping:

- 2 cups fresh strawberries, sliced
- Sugar-free sweetener, to taste
- Whipped cream (unsweetened or sweetened with sugar-free sweetener)

Instructions:

For the Shortcakes:

Preheat your oven to 350°F (175°C). Line a baking sheet with parchment paper.
In a large bowl, whisk together almond flour, coconut flour, sugar-free sweetener, baking powder, baking soda, and salt.
In a separate bowl, whisk together melted butter, eggs, and vanilla extract.
Add the wet ingredients to the dry ingredients and mix until well combined.
Scoop the batter onto the prepared baking sheet to form 6 shortcakes. Shape them with your hands into round, flat discs.
Bake in the preheated oven for 15-18 minutes or until the shortcakes are golden brown and a toothpick inserted into the center comes out clean.
Allow the shortcakes to cool completely before assembling.

For the Topping:

> In a bowl, combine sliced strawberries with sugar-free sweetener to taste. Let them sit for a few minutes to release their juices.
> Slice the cooled shortcakes in half horizontally.
> Spoon the strawberry mixture onto the bottom half of each shortcake.
> Top with a dollop of whipped cream.
> Place the other half of the shortcake on top.
> Optionally, garnish with additional sliced strawberries and a small dollop of whipped cream.
> Serve and enjoy your Sugar-Free Strawberry Shortcake!

This dessert is a delicious, low-sugar alternative to traditional strawberry shortcake, making it suitable for those looking to reduce their sugar intake.

Almond Joy Protein Smoothie

Ingredients:

- 1 cup unsweetened almond milk
- 1 scoop chocolate protein powder
- 2 tablespoons almond butter
- 1 tablespoon unsweetened cocoa powder
- 1 tablespoon shredded coconut (unsweetened)
- 1/2 teaspoon coconut extract
- 1/2 teaspoon vanilla extract
- Ice cubes (optional)
- Sugar-free sweetener to taste (optional)

Instructions:

In a blender, combine the unsweetened almond milk, chocolate protein powder, almond butter, cocoa powder, shredded coconut, coconut extract, and vanilla extract.

If you prefer a colder smoothie, add ice cubes to the blender.

Blend all the ingredients until smooth and creamy. If the smoothie is too thick, you can add more almond milk.

Taste the smoothie and add sugar-free sweetener if needed, depending on your preference.

Blend again to incorporate the sweetener if added.

Pour the Almond Joy Protein Smoothie into a glass and garnish with additional shredded coconut if desired.

Enjoy your delicious and protein-packed smoothie!

This smoothie captures the flavors of an Almond Joy candy bar while providing the benefits of protein from the protein powder and healthy fats from almond butter. Adjust the sweetness and consistency according to your taste preferences.

Pumpkin Spice Chia Pudding

Ingredients:

- 1/4 cup chia seeds
- 1 cup unsweetened almond milk (or any milk of your choice)
- 1/2 cup canned pumpkin puree
- 2-3 tablespoons maple syrup or sweetener of choice (adjust to taste)
- 1/2 teaspoon pumpkin pie spice (or a mixture of cinnamon, nutmeg, and cloves)
- 1/2 teaspoon vanilla extract
- Optional toppings: Chopped nuts, whipped cream, or a sprinkle of cinnamon

Instructions:

In a bowl, whisk together the chia seeds, almond milk, canned pumpkin puree, maple syrup, pumpkin pie spice, and vanilla extract.
Whisk the ingredients thoroughly to ensure that the chia seeds are well distributed.
Let the mixture sit for about 5 minutes, then whisk again to prevent clumping.
Cover the bowl and refrigerate the Pumpkin Spice Chia Pudding for at least 4 hours or overnight, allowing it to thicken.
Before serving, give the pudding a good stir to make sure it has a creamy consistency.
Adjust the sweetness if needed by adding more maple syrup.
Spoon the Pumpkin Spice Chia Pudding into serving bowls or jars.
Optionally, top the pudding with chopped nuts, a dollop of whipped cream, or a sprinkle of cinnamon.
Enjoy your Pumpkin Spice Chia Pudding as a delightful fall-inspired treat!

This chia pudding is not only delicious but also a healthy and fiber-rich option for breakfast or dessert. Adjust the sweetness and spice levels according to your taste preferences.

Raspberry Almond Thumbprint Cookies

Ingredients:

For the Cookies:

- 1 cup almond flour
- 1/4 cup coconut flour
- 1/4 cup unsalted butter, softened
- 1/4 cup sugar or sugar substitute
- 1 large egg
- 1/2 teaspoon almond extract
- 1/4 teaspoon salt

For the Filling:

- 1/4 cup sugar-free raspberry jam or preserves
- Sliced almonds for topping

Instructions:

Preheat your oven to 350°F (175°C). Line a baking sheet with parchment paper.
In a bowl, cream together the softened butter and sugar until light and fluffy.
Add the egg and almond extract to the butter mixture, and beat until well combined.
In a separate bowl, whisk together the almond flour, coconut flour, and salt.
Gradually add the dry ingredients to the wet ingredients, mixing until a dough forms.
Roll the dough into tablespoon-sized balls and place them on the prepared baking sheet.
Use your thumb or the back of a teaspoon to make an indentation in the center of each cookie.
Fill each indentation with about 1/2 teaspoon of sugar-free raspberry jam.
Top each cookie with a few sliced almonds.
Bake in the preheated oven for 10-12 minutes or until the edges are golden brown.

Allow the cookies to cool on the baking sheet for a few minutes before transferring them to a wire rack to cool completely.
Once cooled, the Raspberry Almond Thumbprint Cookies are ready to be enjoyed!

These cookies offer a delightful combination of almond flavor and raspberry sweetness.

Adjust the sweetness level and experiment with different sugar substitutes if desired.

Greek Yogurt Cheesecake Bites

Ingredients:

For the Crust:

- 1 cup almond flour
- 2 tablespoons melted coconut oil or unsalted butter
- 1 tablespoon sugar or sugar substitute

For the Cheesecake Filling:

- 1 cup Greek yogurt (plain or vanilla)
- 8 oz cream cheese, softened
- 1/4 cup sugar or sugar substitute
- 1 teaspoon vanilla extract
- 2 large eggs

For Topping (optional):

- Fresh berries or fruit compote

Instructions:

For the Crust:

Preheat your oven to 350°F (175°C). Line a mini muffin tin with paper liners.
In a bowl, mix together almond flour, melted coconut oil or butter, and sugar until well combined.
Press a small amount of the crust mixture into the bottom of each muffin cup, creating a firm base.
Bake the crusts in the preheated oven for 8-10 minutes or until they are lightly golden. Allow them to cool while you prepare the filling.

For the Cheesecake Filling:

In a mixing bowl, beat the softened cream cheese until smooth.
Add Greek yogurt, sugar or sugar substitute, and vanilla extract to the cream cheese. Mix until well combined.
Add the eggs, one at a time, beating well after each addition.
Spoon the cheesecake filling over the cooled crusts in the muffin tin, filling each cup almost to the top.
Bake in the preheated oven for 15-18 minutes or until the cheesecake bites are set and the edges are lightly golden.
Allow the cheesecake bites to cool in the muffin tin for about 10 minutes, then transfer them to a wire rack to cool completely.

For Topping (optional):

Once cooled, top each cheesecake bite with fresh berries or a fruit compote of your choice.
Refrigerate the Greek Yogurt Cheesecake Bites for at least 2 hours or until fully chilled.
Serve and enjoy your delicious and creamy cheesecake bites!

These Greek Yogurt Cheesecake Bites are a healthier alternative to traditional cheesecake, offering a rich and creamy texture with the added protein from Greek yogurt. Customize them with your favorite toppings.

Matcha Green Tea Energy Balls

Ingredients:

- 1 cup rolled oats
- 1/2 cup almond flour
- 2 tablespoons matcha green tea powder
- 1/2 cup nut butter (such as almond or cashew)
- 1/4 cup honey or maple syrup
- 1 teaspoon vanilla extract
- A pinch of salt
- Optional: Desiccated coconut or sesame seeds for rolling

Instructions:

In a food processor, combine rolled oats, almond flour, and matcha green tea powder. Pulse until the oats are finely ground.
Add the nut butter, honey or maple syrup, vanilla extract, and a pinch of salt to the food processor. Blend until the mixture forms a sticky dough.
If the mixture is too dry, you can add a bit more nut butter or honey to reach the desired consistency.
Scoop out small portions of the mixture and roll them into bite-sized balls using your hands.
Optional: Roll the energy balls in desiccated coconut or sesame seeds for an extra layer of flavor and texture.
Place the energy balls on a parchment-lined tray or plate.
Refrigerate the Matcha Green Tea Energy Balls for at least 30 minutes to firm up.
Once set, transfer the energy balls to an airtight container and store them in the refrigerator.
Enjoy these delicious and energizing Matcha Green Tea Energy Balls as a quick snack or pick-me-up!

These energy balls combine the vibrant flavor of matcha with the goodness of nuts and oats, providing a healthy and satisfying treat. Adjust sweetness and experiment with different coatings according to your preferences.

Chocolate Dipped Apricots

Ingredients:

- Dried apricots (as many as desired)
- 1 cup dark chocolate chips or chopped dark chocolate
- 1 tablespoon coconut oil
- Optional toppings: Chopped nuts, shredded coconut, or sea salt

Instructions:

Line a tray or plate with parchment paper.
In a microwave-safe bowl or using a double boiler, melt the dark chocolate and coconut oil together. If using a microwave, heat in 20-second intervals, stirring between each interval until fully melted.
Dip each dried apricot halfway into the melted chocolate, allowing any excess chocolate to drip off.
Place the chocolate-dipped apricots on the prepared parchment paper.
Optional: Sprinkle chopped nuts, shredded coconut, or a pinch of sea salt on top of the chocolate-dipped apricots before the chocolate sets.
Allow the chocolate to set by placing the tray in the refrigerator for about 15-20 minutes.
Once the chocolate is completely hardened, transfer the Chocolate Dipped Apricots to a serving plate or store them in an airtight container.
Enjoy these delightful and easy-to-make treats!

These Chocolate Dipped Apricots are a quick and delicious way to satisfy your sweet cravings. The combination of rich dark chocolate and sweet dried apricots creates a delightful contrast of flavors. Customize them with your favorite toppings for added texture and flavor.

Low-Sugar Apple Crisp

Ingredients:

For the Filling:

- 6 cups sliced and peeled apples (such as Granny Smith or Honeycrisp)
- 1 tablespoon lemon juice
- 2 tablespoons sugar or sugar substitute (adjust to taste)
- 1 teaspoon ground cinnamon
- 1/4 teaspoon nutmeg (optional)

For the Topping:

- 1 cup old-fashioned oats
- 1/2 cup almond flour or whole wheat flour
- 1/4 cup chopped nuts (such as pecans or walnuts)
- 1/4 cup melted coconut oil or unsalted butter
- 2 tablespoons sugar or sugar substitute
- 1 teaspoon ground cinnamon
- A pinch of salt

Instructions:

Preheat your oven to 350°F (175°C). Grease a baking dish.
In a large bowl, toss the sliced apples with lemon juice, sugar, cinnamon, and nutmeg (if using). Transfer the apple mixture to the prepared baking dish.
In a separate bowl, combine the oats, almond flour or whole wheat flour, chopped nuts, melted coconut oil or butter, sugar, cinnamon, and a pinch of salt. Mix until the topping forms a crumbly texture.
Sprinkle the topping evenly over the apples in the baking dish.
Bake in the preheated oven for 35-40 minutes or until the apples are tender, and the topping is golden brown.
Remove the Low-Sugar Apple Crisp from the oven and let it cool for a few minutes before serving.
Serve warm on its own or with a scoop of low-sugar vanilla ice cream or a dollop of Greek yogurt if desired.
Enjoy this delicious and healthier version of apple crisp with reduced sugar!

This low-sugar apple crisp is a comforting and satisfying dessert that captures the flavors of fall without excessive sweetness. Adjust the sugar content according to your taste preferences.

Coconut Almond Joy Bars

Ingredients:

For the Base:

- 1 cup almond flour
- 1/4 cup coconut flour
- 1/4 cup melted coconut oil
- 2 tablespoons unsweetened shredded coconut
- 2 tablespoons maple syrup or any sweetener of your choice
- A pinch of salt

For the Coconut Filling:

- 2 cups shredded coconut (unsweetened)
- 1/2 cup coconut cream
- 1/4 cup melted coconut oil
- 1/4 cup maple syrup or any sweetener of your choice
- 1 teaspoon vanilla extract
- A pinch of salt

For the Chocolate Topping:

- 1 cup dark chocolate chips or chopped dark chocolate
- 1 tablespoon coconut oil

Instructions:

For the Base:

Line a square or rectangular baking dish with parchment paper, leaving some overhang for easy removal.
In a bowl, mix together almond flour, coconut flour, melted coconut oil, shredded coconut, maple syrup, and a pinch of salt until well combined.
Press the mixture into the bottom of the prepared baking dish to create an even layer. Place it in the freezer while you prepare the coconut filling.

For the Coconut Filling:

In a food processor, combine shredded coconut, coconut cream, melted coconut oil, maple syrup, vanilla extract, and a pinch of salt.
Process the mixture until it becomes a sticky and well-combined filling.
Remove the baking dish from the freezer and spread the coconut filling evenly over the base layer.
Place the baking dish back in the freezer while you prepare the chocolate topping.

For the Chocolate Topping:

In a microwave-safe bowl or using a double boiler, melt the dark chocolate and coconut oil together. Stir until smooth.
Pour the melted chocolate over the coconut filling, spreading it evenly.
Place the baking dish in the refrigerator for at least 2-3 hours or until the bars are set.
Once set, use the parchment paper overhang to lift the Coconut Almond Joy Bars out of the dish.
Place them on a cutting board and use a sharp knife to cut them into squares or bars.
Store the bars in the refrigerator until ready to serve.
Enjoy these delicious and homemade Coconut Almond Joy Bars!

These bars capture the flavors of the classic Almond Joy candy bar with a healthier twist. They're perfect for satisfying your sweet tooth with the combination of coconut, almonds, and dark chocolate. Adjust sweetness and experiment with different sweeteners if desired.

Vanilla Bean Panna Cotta

Ingredients:

- 2 cups heavy cream
- 1/2 cup whole milk
- 1/2 cup granulated sugar
- 1 vanilla bean pod, split lengthwise and seeds scraped (or 1-2 teaspoons vanilla extract)
- 2 1/4 teaspoons unflavored gelatin
- 3 tablespoons cold water

For the Vanilla Bean Sauce (Optional):

- 1/2 cup water
- 1/4 cup granulated sugar
- 1 vanilla bean pod, split lengthwise and seeds scraped (or 1-2 teaspoons vanilla extract)

Instructions:

In a saucepan, combine heavy cream, whole milk, and granulated sugar over medium heat. Add the scraped vanilla bean seeds and the split pod to infuse flavor. Bring the mixture to a gentle simmer, stirring occasionally. Once it simmers, remove it from heat.

In a small bowl, sprinkle gelatin over cold water and let it sit for about 5 minutes to bloom.

Remove the vanilla bean pod from the cream mixture.

Gently reheat the cream mixture over medium heat. Once warmed, add the bloomed gelatin and stir until completely dissolved.

Remove the mixture from heat and let it cool slightly. If you used a vanilla bean pod, remove any remaining seeds with a fine mesh strainer.

Pour the mixture into ramekins or molds. Refrigerate for at least 4 hours or until set.

Optional: For the Vanilla Bean Sauce, combine water, granulated sugar, vanilla bean seeds, and the split pod in a small saucepan. Bring to a simmer over medium heat, stirring until the sugar dissolves. Let it simmer for a few minutes until it slightly thickens. Remove from heat and let it cool.

Once the panna cotta is set, run a knife around the edge of each ramekin and invert onto a serving plate.
Drizzle with the Vanilla Bean Sauce if desired.
Serve and enjoy your Vanilla Bean Panna Cotta!

This Vanilla Bean Panna Cotta is a silky and elegant dessert with the delightful flavor of vanilla. It can be served on its own or with a sauce of your choice, such as fresh berries or a caramel sauce. Adjust the sweetness and vanilla intensity according to your preferences.

Chocolate Almond Butter Banana Bites

Ingredients:

- 2 large bananas, peeled and sliced into rounds
- 2 tablespoons almond butter
- 1/2 cup dark chocolate chips
- 1 teaspoon coconut oil
- Optional toppings: Chopped nuts, shredded coconut, or sea salt

Instructions:

Line a tray or plate with parchment paper.
Spread a small amount of almond butter on one side of each banana round and create banana "sandwiches" by placing another banana round on top.
In a microwave-safe bowl or using a double boiler, melt the dark chocolate chips and coconut oil together. Stir until smooth.
Dip each banana bite into the melted chocolate, coating it halfway or completely, depending on your preference.
Place the chocolate-coated banana bites on the prepared parchment paper.
Optional: Sprinkle chopped nuts, shredded coconut, or a pinch of sea salt on top of the chocolate coating before it sets.
Repeat the process for all banana bites.
Place the tray in the refrigerator for about 30 minutes or until the chocolate coating hardens.
Once set, transfer the Chocolate Almond Butter Banana Bites to a serving plate.
Serve and enjoy these delightful and satisfying bites!

These Chocolate Almond Butter Banana Bites make for a delicious and healthier dessert or snack. The combination of creamy almond butter, sweet bananas, and rich dark chocolate is sure to satisfy your sweet cravings. Customize them with your favorite toppings or add-ins.

Berry Yogurt Popsicles

Ingredients:

- 1 cup mixed berries (strawberries, blueberries, raspberries)
- 1 cup Greek yogurt (plain or vanilla)
- 2 tablespoons honey or maple syrup (adjust to taste)
- 1 teaspoon vanilla extract
- 1/2 cup milk (almond milk, coconut milk, or any milk of your choice)

Instructions:

In a blender, combine mixed berries, Greek yogurt, honey or maple syrup, vanilla extract, and milk.
Blend the ingredients until smooth and well combined. Taste the mixture and adjust sweetness if needed.
Pour the berry yogurt mixture into popsicle molds, leaving a little space at the top for expansion.
Insert popsicle sticks into the molds.
Freeze the popsicles for at least 4-6 hours or until completely set.
Once frozen, run the popsicle molds under warm water for a few seconds to help release the popsicles.
Remove the Berry Yogurt Popsicles from the molds and enjoy!

These Berry Yogurt Popsicles are not only delicious but also a healthy and refreshing treat, perfect for a hot day or as a wholesome dessert. Feel free to customize the recipe with your favorite berries or add a layer of granola for extra texture.

Cinnamon Raisin Protein Cookies

Ingredients:

- 1 cup rolled oats
- 1 cup vanilla protein powder
- 1 teaspoon ground cinnamon
- 1/2 teaspoon baking powder
- 1/4 teaspoon salt
- 1/2 cup almond butter
- 1/4 cup honey or maple syrup
- 1 large egg
- 1 teaspoon vanilla extract
- 1/2 cup raisins

Instructions:

Preheat your oven to 350°F (175°C). Line a baking sheet with parchment paper.
In a blender or food processor, pulse the rolled oats until they form a fine flour-like consistency.
In a large mixing bowl, combine the oat flour, vanilla protein powder, ground cinnamon, baking powder, and salt.
In a separate microwave-safe bowl, heat the almond butter for about 20-30 seconds until it becomes easier to mix.
Add the melted almond butter, honey or maple syrup, egg, and vanilla extract to the dry ingredients. Mix until well combined.
Fold in the raisins into the cookie dough.
Scoop out tablespoon-sized portions of the dough and roll them into balls. Place them on the prepared baking sheet, spacing them about 2 inches apart.
Use a fork to flatten each cookie slightly.
Bake in the preheated oven for 10-12 minutes or until the edges are golden brown.
Allow the cookies to cool on the baking sheet for a few minutes before transferring them to a wire rack to cool completely.
Once cooled, enjoy your Cinnamon Raisin Protein Cookies!

These protein cookies are not only delicious but also packed with the goodness of oats, protein, and natural sweetness from raisins. Adjust the sweetness level according to your preference and feel free to experiment with different protein powders.

Avocado Lime Sorbet

Ingredients:

- 2 ripe avocados, peeled and pitted
- 1 cup coconut milk (or any milk of your choice)
- 1/2 cup honey or maple syrup (adjust to taste)
- Zest and juice of 2 limes
- 1/2 teaspoon vanilla extract

Instructions:

In a blender, combine the ripe avocados, coconut milk, honey or maple syrup, lime zest, lime juice, and vanilla extract.
Blend the ingredients until smooth and creamy.
Taste the mixture and adjust the sweetness by adding more honey or maple syrup if needed.
Pour the avocado lime mixture into an ice cream maker and churn according to the manufacturer's instructions until it reaches a sorbet-like consistency.
If you don't have an ice cream maker, pour the mixture into a shallow dish and place it in the freezer.
Every 30 minutes, stir the mixture with a fork to break up ice crystals. Repeat this process for about 3-4 hours or until the sorbet is firm and scoopable.
Once the Avocado Lime Sorbet reaches the desired consistency, transfer it to an airtight container and store it in the freezer.
Serve the sorbet in bowls or cones and enjoy this refreshing and creamy treat!

This Avocado Lime Sorbet is a unique and dairy-free dessert that combines the creamy texture of avocados with the bright and zesty flavor of lime. Adjust the sweetness and lime intensity according to your taste preferences.

Walnut Dark Chocolate Clusters

Ingredients:

- 1 cup dark chocolate chips or chopped dark chocolate
- 1 cup walnut halves or pieces
- 1 tablespoon coconut oil
- 1/2 teaspoon vanilla extract
- A pinch of sea salt (optional)

Instructions:

Line a tray or plate with parchment paper.
In a microwave-safe bowl or using a double boiler, melt the dark chocolate and coconut oil together. Stir until smooth.
Stir in the vanilla extract and a pinch of sea salt, if desired.
Add the walnut halves or pieces to the melted chocolate, making sure they are well coated.
Spoon clusters of the chocolate-coated walnuts onto the prepared parchment paper. You can make them as small or large as you prefer.
Optional: Sprinkle a little extra sea salt on top of each cluster for a sweet and salty combination.
Allow the Walnut Dark Chocolate Clusters to set by placing the tray in the refrigerator for about 30 minutes.
Once set, transfer the clusters to an airtight container and store them in the refrigerator.
Enjoy these delightful and easy-to-make Walnut Dark Chocolate Clusters as a delicious treat!

These clusters are a perfect combination of rich dark chocolate and crunchy walnuts. Customize them by adding dried fruits, shredded coconut, or a sprinkle of your favorite spices for added flavor.

Peach Yogurt Parfait

Ingredients:

- 2 cups Greek yogurt (plain or vanilla)
- 2 ripe peaches, peeled and diced
- 1 cup granola (store-bought or homemade)
- 2 tablespoons honey or maple syrup
- 1/4 cup sliced almonds or your favorite nuts (optional)

Instructions:

In serving glasses or bowls, layer 1/4 cup of Greek yogurt at the bottom.
Add a layer of diced peaches on top of the yogurt.
Sprinkle a layer of granola over the peaches.
Drizzle honey or maple syrup over the granola layer.
Repeat the layers until you reach the top of the glass or bowl.
Optionally, top the parfait with sliced almonds or your favorite nuts for added crunch.
Repeat the process for additional parfaits.
Serve immediately and enjoy your refreshing Peach Yogurt Parfait!

This Peach Yogurt Parfait is not only visually appealing but also a delightful combination of creamy yogurt, sweet peaches, crunchy granola, and a touch of honey. Feel free to customize it with your favorite fruits, nuts, or additional toppings.

No-Bake Hazelnut Energy Bites

Ingredients:

- 1 cup rolled oats
- 1/2 cup hazelnuts, toasted and chopped
- 1/2 cup almond butter
- 1/3 cup honey or maple syrup
- 1/4 cup unsweetened cocoa powder
- 1 teaspoon vanilla extract
- A pinch of salt
- Optional: Shredded coconut for rolling

Instructions:

In a dry skillet over medium heat, toast the hazelnuts for 5-7 minutes or until fragrant. Stir frequently to prevent burning. Once toasted, let them cool and then chop them.
In a large mixing bowl, combine rolled oats, chopped hazelnuts, almond butter, honey or maple syrup, cocoa powder, vanilla extract, and a pinch of salt.
Mix the ingredients thoroughly until a sticky dough forms.
If the mixture is too wet, you can add more oats. If it's too dry, add a bit more almond butter or honey.
Optional: Place shredded coconut in a separate bowl.
Scoop out small portions of the mixture and roll them into bite-sized balls using your hands.
Optional: Roll the energy bites in shredded coconut for an extra layer of flavor.
Place the energy bites on a parchment-lined tray or plate.
Refrigerate the No-Bake Hazelnut Energy Bites for at least 30 minutes to firm up.
Once set, transfer the energy bites to an airtight container and store them in the refrigerator.
Enjoy these delicious and energy-boosting Hazelnut Energy Bites as a quick snack!

These no-bake energy bites are a convenient and tasty way to incorporate hazelnuts into your diet. They are packed with the goodness of nuts, oats, and cocoa, making them a satisfying and nutritious snack. Adjust sweetness and experiment with different coatings according to your preferences.

Blueberry Cheesecake Bites

Ingredients:

For the Crust:

- 1 cup almond flour
- 2 tablespoons melted coconut oil or unsalted butter
- 1 tablespoon sugar or sugar substitute

For the Cheesecake Filling:

- 8 oz cream cheese, softened
- 1/4 cup sugar or sugar substitute
- 1 teaspoon vanilla extract
- 1 large egg

For the Blueberry Topping:

- 1/2 cup fresh blueberries
- 1 tablespoon water
- 1 tablespoon sugar or sugar substitute
- 1 teaspoon lemon juice

Instructions:

For the Crust:

Preheat your oven to 350°F (175°C). Line a mini muffin tin with paper liners.
In a bowl, mix together almond flour, melted coconut oil or butter, and sugar until well combined.
Press a small amount of the crust mixture into the bottom of each muffin cup, creating a firm base.
Bake the crusts in the preheated oven for 8-10 minutes or until they are lightly golden. Allow them to cool while you prepare the filling.

For the Cheesecake Filling:

In a mixing bowl, beat the softened cream cheese until smooth.
Add sugar or sugar substitute and vanilla extract to the cream cheese. Mix until well combined.
Add the egg, beating well after its addition.
Spoon the cheesecake filling over the cooled crusts in the muffin tin, filling each cup almost to the top.

For the Blueberry Topping:

In a small saucepan, combine blueberries, water, sugar or sugar substitute, and lemon juice.
Simmer the mixture over medium heat, stirring occasionally, until the blueberries soften and release their juices. This should take about 5 minutes.
Mash some of the blueberries with a fork to create a sauce-like consistency.
Spoon the blueberry topping over the cheesecake filling in each muffin cup.
Bake in the preheated oven for 12-15 minutes or until the cheesecake is set and the edges are slightly golden.
Allow the Blueberry Cheesecake Bites to cool in the muffin tin for about 10 minutes, then transfer them to a wire rack to cool completely.
Once cooled, refrigerate the bites for at least 2 hours or until fully chilled.
Serve and enjoy these delightful Blueberry Cheesecake Bites!

These mini cheesecake bites are a perfect combination of creamy cheesecake, almond crust, and a burst of blueberry flavor. Adjust sweetness and experiment with different sugar substitutes if desired.

Chia Seed Chocolate Pudding

Ingredients:

- 1/4 cup chia seeds
- 1 cup milk (almond milk, coconut milk, or any milk of your choice)
- 2 tablespoons cocoa powder
- 2-3 tablespoons honey or maple syrup (adjust to taste)
- 1/2 teaspoon vanilla extract
- A pinch of salt

Optional Toppings:

- Fresh berries
- Sliced bananas
- Chopped nuts
- Shredded coconut

Instructions:

In a bowl, whisk together chia seeds, milk, cocoa powder, honey or maple syrup, vanilla extract, and a pinch of salt.
Whisk the ingredients thoroughly to ensure that the chia seeds are well distributed.
Let the mixture sit for about 5 minutes, then whisk again to prevent clumping.
Cover the bowl and refrigerate the Chia Seed Chocolate Pudding for at least 4 hours or overnight, allowing it to thicken.
Before serving, give the pudding a good stir to make sure it has a creamy consistency.
Adjust the sweetness if needed by adding more honey or maple syrup.
Spoon the Chia Seed Chocolate Pudding into serving bowls or jars.
Optional: Top the pudding with fresh berries, sliced bananas, chopped nuts, or shredded coconut for added texture and flavor.
Enjoy your delicious and nutritious Chia Seed Chocolate Pudding!

This chocolate pudding is not only rich and satisfying but also packed with the health benefits of chia seeds. It makes for a delightful dessert or a healthy snack. Feel free to customize the toppings according to your preferences.